Asthma

By Jillian Powell

Contents

WHAT'S WRONG?

If you have asthma, it is sometimes hard to breathe normally. Your chest may feel tight and you may feel short of breath. Sometimes you start coughing and wheezing. This is called having an **asthma attack**.

Did you know?
One in seven children have asthma.

Lewis's story

I had my first asthma attack when I was six. It was a bit scary because I had to go to the hospital. But the doctors soon made me feel better.

Dear Doc

What are the best foods to eat if you have asthma?

Eat plenty of fresh fruit and vegetables to boost your immune system.

WHAT'S GOING ON?

When you breathe air into your nose or mouth, it goes through the **airways** into your **lungs**. If you have asthma, the airways can narrow so there is less room for air to get through. Sometimes they fill with **mucus**. This can make you cough and wheeze.

Did you know?
Babies and children breathe much faster than adults.

WHAT CAUSES ASTHMA?

Everyone's asthma is different. Often, a cold or another **virus** can bring it on. Other common **asthma triggers** are cold air, smoke, dust, **pollution,** and plant **pollen**. Some people get asthma if they eat certain foods, or if they go near pets.

Dear Doc

My mom and I both get asthma. Will my brother get it too?

Asthma can run in families, so it is more likely, but not certain that he will get it too.

I used to have a cat called Flo, but I got a really bad asthma attack when I was playing with her one day. After that, Mom said we had to find her a new home.

Rachel's story

I use my preventer inhaler before I brush my teeth in the morning and at night. Brushing my teeth helps wash out any medicine left in my mouth.

12

ASTHMA MEDICINE

If you have asthma, you can take medicine to help you breathe more easily. You use an inhaler to breathe medicine into your airways and lungs. Some people need to use a **preventer inhaler** every day. This helps to keep their airways open.

Did you know?
Smoking and *passive smoking* make asthma worse.

ASTHMA ATTACKS

If you have an asthma attack, you may need to use a **reliever inhaler**. This helps to open your airways so it becomes easier to breathe. A **spacer** can help to get more of the medicine down into your lungs. If your asthma gets worse you may need to take pills or liquid medicine too.

14

Dear Doc

How can I avoid having an asthma attack?

Keep a diary of your asthma triggers so that you can try to avoid them.

Alice's story

I carry my reliever inhaler and spacer with me everywhere. It's a different color from the preventer inhaler, so I don't mix the two of them up!

LIVING WITH ASTHMA

You can use a **peak flow meter** every day. This will tell you how well you are breathing and if you need to use a preventer inhaler. You can help to prevent asthma attacks by avoiding triggers such as dusty or smoky rooms.

Dear Doc

How do I know if my asthma is getting better or worse?

You can keep a peak flow meter diary. It will help your doctor too.

CHECKUPS

If you have asthma, you will need to have regular check-ups with a doctor or nurse. They will weigh and measure you and ask you to blow into a peak flow meter. They will also advise you how to avoid your asthma triggers.

18

Dear Doc

My asthma is worse in cold weather. What can I do?

Pull your scarf up over your nose and mouth to warm the air you breathe in.

19

EXERCISE AND ASTHMA

Playing sports helps exercise the lungs and airways. They also boost your immune system. Swimming is good as the warm, damp air can help your airways stay open. Avoid exercising outdoors in cold, dry weather, as this can be an asthma trigger.

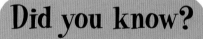

Did you know?

Some famous sports stars like Isaiah Thomas have asthma.

Harvey's story

Sometimes grass pollen brings my asthma on when I play soccer. I always take my reliever inhaler with me. If I have an asthma attack, I have to rest a bit.

Glossary

Airways	the tubes that carry air from the nose or mouth to the lungs
Asthma attack	when asthma affects you badly
Asthma trigger	something that upsets the airways and brings on an asthma attack
Immune system	parts of the body that fight infection
Lungs	parts of the body that we use for breathing
Mucus	sticky stuff made in the body, also called phlegm
Passive smoking	when someone breathes in smoke from another person's cigarette
Peak flow meter	a device that shows how hard someone can blow out air
Pollen	powder produced by plants so that they can reproduce
Pollution	dirt and chemicals from cars and factories
Preventer inhaler	a device for taking medicine to help keep the airways open
Reliever inhaler	a device for taking medicine to open the airways during an asthma attack
Spacer	a device that can be used with an inhaler to help get more of the medicine down into the lungs
Virus	a germ that multiplies inside body cells